No Sweat Home Schooling

The Low stress Way
To Teach Your Kids

By
Kelly Wallace

What Readers Are Saying:

"The resources alone are worth the low cost of this excellent book! It saved me the trouble of hunting online for these excellent websites myself." - Anna C.

"Solid guidance for new and established homeschooling families." - David R.

"I've read a lot of homeschooling books before, but this is by far the best yet. Down-to-earth, practical, even humorous at times. It really helped me to feel that there was a kindred spirit in the world who went through what I'm going through now. I have no doubt that I made the right decision to homeschool my sons!" - Barbara N.

"Different and enlightening. Two thumbs up!" - Michelle B.

"I'd pay ten times as much for this book. Wonderful in every way!" - Christine A.

"I felt like the author was an old friend holding my hand until I was more confident and could walk alone on this homeschooling path." - Susan C.

"This book takes the confusion out of whether or not to homeschool and how to do it with minimal stress and frustration. Ms. Wallace has made homeschooling fun for myself and my kids!" Anita R.

Disclaimer

All information contained in this publication reflects the personal views of the author at the time of publication. While the author has made reasonable efforts to ensure the accuracy of the information contained herein, it is possible that typographical or contextual errors have been made or that information has changed since the date of publication.

The author shall not be held liable or responsible to any person or entity regarding loss or damage caused by, or allegedly caused by, the information contained in this book either directly or indirectly. The purchaser/reader acknowledges that the author has compiled this book for general informational only, and is not engaged in offering legal, financial, or other professional services or advice.

Table Of Contents

Introduction

I was a homeschooling mom for over a decade. During that time I learned a lot along the way, made lots of mistakes, eventually did things right and have written many articles on the subject of schooling from home for top sites such as Suite101, Families, Yahoo, and more. In this book I'd like to share some of these articles (expanded and updated), and a bit about myself and my background as a homeschooling single mother. I'll cover subjects such as whole curriculum subjects, frugal field trips, record keeping, fun activities, pitfalls, stress busters and more. I also include a lot of quality online resources.

The decision to home school your kids is one you'll never regret, though the path can often be confusing, frustrating and lonely. It's my goal to be honest and open with my worries and fears and ultimate victories so you can see you aren't alone. There are days when you'll be absolutely certain you made the worst decision of your life, and days when you feel like you've finally gotten the hang of it and know you'd done the right thing. Being able to teach your own children in accordance with your personal morals, values, goals, and ideals is a wonderful thing!

Within these pages I'll offer some of my opinions and experiences and hope you'll run with them and create your own homeschool curriculum and routine. This isn't a step-by-step guide to follow, but is instead a low stress way to teach your kids and be certain they're actually retaining what they learn. Consider this short book an appetizer to whet your appetite regarding homeschooling. Something to get your own creative juices flowing so you can try out some of these ideas and add plenty of your own to create the type of education you want for your children.

I truly believe that homeschooling should be as much fun for you as it is for them. After all, you'll be spending many hours each week together learning new things. Why make it bland and boring? Instead, with a bit of ingenuity you can turn even the smallest everyday task into a learning opportunity that sticks with your children for years to come.

A Note From The Author

As you read through this book you may notice that I repeat some things. The reason for this is that some people may not read the book straight through and will skip around to the areas they prefer to read about.

Also, I noticed that I used the word "stress", "stressed", or "stressful" over thirty times. Yes, homeschooling can be stressful! And that's why I wrote this book, so you can learn to teach your kids easily the no-sweat way. I wish I would have had this very book 15 years ago when I started my homeschooling journey. It would have saved me a lot of time and frustration.

As you read the book take what you like, leave the rest, and come back to it another time if you want to. It's meant to spark your own interest and curiosity, not to be a blue-print for you to follow word-for-word. Though, if you did, you'd still do just fine, and far better than if you simply groped around in the dark or stuck to dull and dry curriculum packages. I hope that over the coming months and years you'll come back to your copy of *No Sweat Home Schooling* again and again.

Now, let's dive right in!

My Journey In A Nutshell

Out of my five daughters, the two oldest went to public school all the way through high school. A move from California to a rough area of Baltimore had me quickly pulling my two younger daughters right out of school and homeschooling them myself. My youngest never went to public school. It was a decision I wish I had made with my older girls. Live and learn though, right?

For the most part I used the Charlotte Mason method of homeschooling, but I also incorporated some of my own ideas such a "whole curriculum" or "across the curriculum" art, history, or social studies lessons. Being a frugal person who values both time and money, I needed to get the most education I could out of everything we tackled.

About 6 years after I started homeschooling my girls I was divorced for the second time. Although my nerves were just about frazzled beyond all hope, I simply tied them in a knot on top of my head and went about my life. Having the kids home all the time did contribute to a bit more mess, but we have memories that could never be replaced had I sent them to public school.

Along this path I was also a work-at-home mom. I didn't want it any other way and couldn't see any other way to make our lives work. If I had a 9-to-5 job then who would watch my kids and be their teacher? I surely wasn't sending them back to public school, which I aptly called "Kiddy Prison." Like all self-proclaimed Super Moms, I found a way to make it all work.

The level of education my girls received compared to their public schooled friends is beyond anything I could have imagined. We simply did what was fun and interesting, and things that were logical and necessary. For any parent who has home schooled, I'm sure you know the joys—and pitfalls—of being parent and educator to your children. And for those parents who are thinking about homeschooling but aren't quite sure about it, let me tell you that it's the most rewarding journey you will ever take with your kids. You have a front row center seat as you watch them blossom and grow.

I look forward to sharing my experiences as a homeschooling parent with you!

My Decision To Homeschool

When people find out that my three youngest girls were all home schooled they look at me with something akin to both shock and admiration. They then ask why I decided to do it. I talked a bit about my decision to homeschool in the previous section, but there's more to it than that. Then again, why do we feel we need a reason to homeschool? Do our kids need to be picked on daily or ignored by teachers or taught things we don't agree with just so we have a "real" reason to teach them from home? No, but that's how we're made to feel.

The reason I chose to pull my two third graders out of public school and never let my youngest step foot in a classroom was simply because I felt I was sending them off to a penitentiary each day.

We moved to Baltimore and found a place in what ended up being a pretty rough area. (Now I do a lot of research before I move anywhere!) I didn't think much about it at the time though after growing up in various parts of Los Angeles and never having a bit of trouble. I loved the townhouse we lived in and the scenery of Baltimore was beautiful. It quickly became apparent though that "Dorothy wasn't in Kansas any longer."

My children were picked on, ridiculed and threatened on a daily basis. The classrooms were awful with the obedient children being punished right along with the vast majority of the troublemakers. My kids would often go without lunch and there was never any free time on the playground because, "Too many fights break out," I was told by one teacher. And these were third graders!

No matter how many times I went to the school to talk with the principal and teachers, I'd just hear the same excuses over and over again. When one of my daughters had a knife pulled on her due to the fact that she had blonde hair, they never went back to public school again.

Of course, my story may be extreme, but it's real nonetheless. Top that all off with my girls learning things they had taken when in first grade while living in California, and I knew I had done the right thing by pulling them out of public school.

No, not all public schools are as terrible as the one in my story here, but too many are. Even if the children were all well behaved and got along perfectly, the fact remained that they were getting a sub-par education. There was no way they'd be prepared for the real word!

Has homeschooling truly made a difference? You bet! My two oldest girls went to public school from kindergarten through high school while we lived in California. Back then I trusted that they were learning all they should in order to live independent, stable lives. Instead, it's my three youngest who have lucked out. I know that if they needed to, even years ago at their young ages, they could make it on their own. They could obtain full time jobs, know how to pay bills, budget money, and be frugal. Their knowledge is also vast. They can tell a Van Gogh from a Renoir, know about cultures most children have never heard of, and have read many of the great classics.

Although I started homeschooling just to save my children from potential harm, it was a blessing in disguise. I'm forever grateful to have had the opportunity to not only be their mother, but their educator and mentor as well.

As I mentioned, though the circumstances behind my decision to homeschool my girls was extreme, you don't need anything this shocking to switch from public schooling to homeschooling. Once you make the decision to do it and actually dive right into it, you'll quickly find that it simply feels good and right. Why trust strangers to be your children's teachers? Shouldn't you be the one to guide them? After all, you know what's important to you and your family and what you'd like your kids to learn so they can lead independent, successful lives!

It's Cheaper To Homeschool

Need more reasons to switch from public to homeschooling? How about putting thousands of dollars in your bank account rather than into the public school system? I never realized just how expensive it was to send five kids to school, until I really sat down and did the math.

Back when I was a kid public school was free. Each child got their books, pencils, paper, art supplies, and many other school supplies at no cost. We'd even go on several field trips throughout the year, all for free as well. About the only thing my parents had to pay for was my lunch.

Times have definitely changed. When my girls were still in public school they'd be sent home with a long list of items they needed for the year. Even if you bought most of the items from the dollar store, multiplying that by several children equals a hefty bill. A lot of schools also require uniforms now as well. Add this in with the cost of books you're sometimes required to buy and it's enough to make any parent on a tight budget feel nauseated. It's like choosing between spending your money on school supplies or groceries for a month or more!

I went online to find a sample school list and this is what I found for the current school year:

Grades Six, Seven and Eight -

Supplies needed for the first day of school:

1. Six - 1 subject spiral (at least 100 pages) regular rule notebooks
2. Two - 1 subject spiral 80 page regular rule notebooks
3. Ten - pocket folders
4. One dozen erasable pens (blue or black ink only)
5. One dozen regular pens (blue or black ink only)
6. Three dozen pencils #2
7. Two-Wireless note composition 3 whole punch notebooks
8. One - Three-fold (36 inches by 48 inches) Presentation Board (Science Fair)
9. One - Casio Scientific Calculator to be kept at home for math homework
10. One - 12 inch ruler (preferably with metric measurement also included)
11. One - Box of Tissues
12. One - Flash Drive/ Memory Stick (1GB memory) - with lanyard

Required for the spring English research paper:
* 1 package of 100 lined 3 x 5 Index Cards
* 1 package of 100 lined 4 x 6 Index Cards
* 1 plastic or heavyweight (expanding accordion) folder to hold materials
* 2 highlighters

Not all of these supplies can be purchased at the dollar store, though many could. Even so, if you have several kids in school this will really eat into your budget. At one time I had four kids in school at once and it cost me at least $500 just to buy all of their school supplies and uniforms. How many people, especially in this bad economy, have that kind of money?

Sure, there are programs that will give children of low-income families free school supplies, but there are so many people on their waiting lists that there's no guarantee you'll get the help you need. A lot of families might not be considered low-income, but don't have enough cash all at once to purchase these items before school starts.

Field trips have just about been cut from public schools.

Homeschooling is much cheaper, especially if you put together your own curriculum, as I did. Supplies can be purchased throughout the year rather than all at once, and many everyday tasks can be turned into learning experiences. You can also take your children on several field trips throughout the year that are low-cost or even no-cost.

From a financial standpoint alone, it makes sense to homeschool.

Six Ways To Homeschool

There are so many ways you can homeschool your children, and every family will--and should--have their own unique approach to educational styles and techniques. After all, no two families are alike and your ideals may be different than another family's.

Here are a few things I've tried over the years with my kids:

1. Structured Course Content

I found that a packaged curriculum saved me a lot of time since it's preplanned. I bought most of curriculums online. The lessons can take an hour to five or more. There are also DVD programs you can buy that have an entire year's worth of lessons. The pros were that it saved time. I didn't have to spend hours each week creating my own lesson plans. The cons were that most of these programs are expensive, especially if you get computer software. The books alone can easily cost a couple hundred dollars. There are some websites that sell used curriculums though, so if you prefer having your kids' lessons preplanned then this is a good route for you. I used some workbooks, especially for math lessons, but preferred creating my own lesson plans.

Some of the most popular homeschool curriculums are listed below. I chose only the ones that offered K-12 material (Calvert goes up to grade 8) and had both textbooks and workbooks. Also, I didn't list curriculums that are done only online. Kids are usually on the computer too much as it is! The problem I found was that nearly all homeschool curriculums were solely Christian based and we're a secular (non-religious) family. At present, there are more and more secular based homeschool curriculums available.

The problem I found with every curriculum package was the price. If you're on a budget, homeschooling one child this way is expensive enough, yet alone if you have more kids.

Christian Homeschool Curriculums -

A Beka
Alpha Omega
BJU Press
Christian Liberty
Saxon

For a more detailed list of Christian homeschool curriculums and other resources check out:
ExploringHomeschooling.com

Secular Homeschool Curriculums -

Calvert (PreK through 8th grade)
Connect The Thoughts
Oak Meadow
Progress Academy

For a more detailed list of secular homeschool curriculums and other resources check out:
SecularHomeschool.com

2. Creating Your Own Course Content

Here you'll need to be careful and check the laws of your individual state. Some states require that you include science, math, language arts, and civic studies or history in your curriculum and devote time to each of them on a daily basis. (I got around this by having one subject daily, but using it as "whole curriculum" lessons. More on that later in the book.)

Creating a curriculum by yourself will require you to do some research and find out what your children should be learning for their appropriate age and grade. This method is the most cost effective and makes the best use of your children's capabilities since it can be tailored according to their strengths and weaknesses. I was never one to force a square peg into a round hole and didn't like a cookie cutter approach to teaching my children. They were all different and unique and had their own learning styles. By creating my own course content each and every one of my kids could blossom and grow at their own pace.

The best resource I found for books is Amazon.com. I typically purchased used books and saved a lot of money this way. If you tend to order a lot of books and supplies from Amazon you might want to become an Amazon Prime member. It's only $80 per year and you get free two day shipping on all of your items. It also allows you to borrow books for free (but only one per month) and you can stream movies and TV shows as well.

Also, keep your eyes open for library book sales. These can offer a wide variety of wonderful books you can use for homeschooling and for pennies on the dollar.

3. Online Public School

Many public schools have their own curriculums and materials available online for parents who wish to homeschool. When I was homeschooling my girls this wasn't available then, but my sister uses it and loves it. You'll have to check with your individual state to find out what they offer, but try the K12 website. It probably has all the information you need and you can get started quickly. Best of all, it's free.

K12 - Online Public Schools

4. Online Private School

There are several private online homeschools available, though many can be quite expensive. The positives about this type of schooling is that your children will learn along with many other students who are also enrolled in the online classes and a teacher will guide them online or over the phone. I'm not too keen on this since it reminds me of public school where there's the standard teacher and classmates. Even so, many parents feel comfortable with this more traditional approach. For a list of online private schools, the K12 website has several links and information.

K12 - Online Private Schools

5. Unschooling

This style of teaching takes into account your child's interest in a particular topic and the curriculum is actually led by the child. The term "unschooling" was coined by John Holt in the 1970's. How does it work? Let's say your child is interested in Ancient Greece. You could teach him from books, let him watch educational movies and documentaries on the subject, take him to a museum that has Ancient Greek artifacts, do some art projects, and continue on with the topic until your child is ready to move to something else. I used this a lot with my girls.

A few good resources for unschooling are:

The Unschooler's Emporium
50 Best Blogs In The Unschooling Movement
The Unschooler Experiment

6. An Educational Advocate

An educational advocate will work with you and your children to formulate a curriculum, and some even plan field trips as part of homeschooling to enhance learning. Your children's progress will be monitored by educational consultants. I myself never used an educational advocate since my kids and I did alright on our own. However, for parents that want more structure and direction, this could be a good avenue.

HSLDA (Homeschool advocate site listing laws, news, support groups and more by state.)

Whichever learning path or combination of paths you choose for your children, don't be afraid to experiment over time. If something doesn't work then try something else. If parts of it work but not others, then keep what's working and incorporate another avenue you'd like to try. The worst thing you could do for your kids is box them in with a curriculum they get bored with or hate doing. Sure, no kid will love every lesson or assignment, but homeschooling should be a fun and sometimes daring adventure for you both.

Less Stress In Your Days

As a homeschooling parent you'll quickly find that the hours in each day seem to shrink at a shocking rate. Between housework, errands, perhaps an at-home job, or a baby to take care of, it can be tough to always be in the right frame of mind for the day's lessons. This is why so many parents choose to send their kids back to public school. They simply can't find the time and energy to do all that has to be done. Sometimes you'll have to exchange quantity for quality and get an hour or two of really important activities in with your kids, but there are some tips to staying on track, being more productive, and having less stress in your days.

Daily Planning -

By planning your day in advance you'll always be on top of things and will be able to accomplish so much more than you thought possible. While homeschooling my girls I'd often fluctuate between planning everything to the T or just seizing the day as it came. I have to admit though, by planning ahead I felt more in control and I got much more done. It doesn't take a lot of time to plan ahead either. I would simply get my notebook out and make a list of what needed to be done the following day. This included everything from laundry and shopping to homeschool lessons.

I tried not to set time limits on anything though. Whenever I would put activities into their own little time block I found that it stressed me out a lot more than if I just went down the list. I'd begin my list with what I wanted to accomplish first then end it with what I hoped to get done at the end of the day. I would then put an asterisk next to the things that absolutely had to be done and if they did get completed I was a happy camper. If I also had time to get the less important things done, I was darn near ecstatic! Having at least some sort of structure will help to make your days less stressful.

Remain Flexible -

While it's very helpful to plan ahead and have your daily to-do list, you also want to remain flexible. Sometimes you wake up and the morning somehow gets away from you--perhaps one of your kids is sick, you get an important phone call, you have to take the dog to the vet because he got into the trash and is puking all over the carpet. When this happens look at your list of things you wanted to get done for the day and try not to stress too much about it. Choose what's truly important and what you're comfortably capable of doing with the remaining hours in the day.

If you know you'll have an upcoming appointment you can get to your children's school lessons earlier so you're finished before you need to leave for your appointment. Or, if the appointment is early enough in the day you could always have school lessons when you get back. However, I've found that after being out at the doctor, dentist, running errands, or what have you with the kids, I didn't feel like jumping into school activities when I got home. So, I always scheduled outside activities, field trips, and appointments for the late afternoon.

Then again, you may have days--however few and far between--

when you've got energy to spare and you get housework, school lessons, and a few other things done well before you imagined you would. When this happens, resist the urge to shove more into your day and allow yourself the luxury to do something you enjoy while the kids watch a movie or play. The less stress and pressure you're under, the better you'll be as a homeschooling parent.

Keeping Younger Ones Busy -

When I started homeschooling my youngest was three years old and I tossed her right into the learning lessons along with my older girls. Of course, I made the lessons age-appropriate, but it was easier to homeschool everyone at once rather than trying to cater to each child individually all the time. Also, since my youngest got a head start on schooling she excelled at an incredible rate.

When I had something to do and couldn't be right there for the kids, such as cooking dinner or going over the monthly bills, I'd let the older girls teach their younger sister. They had fun playing teacher since it made them feel grownup and boosted their self-esteem and confidence levels as well.

Although I'm not an advocate of setting kids in front of the TV for hours at a time, I would sometimes put in an educational DVD that my youngest enjoyed, such as Sesame Street, Richard Scarry, or Blue's Clues.

Shorter Lessons -

Something that really helped to keep my kids' attention was shorter lessons. Before I decided to go this route we'd spend an hour or sometimes longer on a subject and I found that my girls quickly lost interest and usually started acting up. Someone would give the other "that look", they'd squirm in their chairs, someone would get poked in the arm with a pencil, papers kept mysteriously falling on the floor...you get the picture.

Once their focus was lost it would be hard to rein it in again. By keeping the lessons to 15-30 minutes we got a lot more done, the children enjoyed the time more, retained much more information, and I felt a whole lot less frustrated. As they got older I increased lesson times accordingly, though many times a half hour is all that's needed. I wanted homeschooling to be enjoyable, not pure drudgery for any of us.

One-On-One Time -

If you're homeschooling multiple children it's important that you set aside one-on-one time with each child. Although you might not be able to do it every day, scheduling in one child per day or every other day works too. Since I was schooling three kids at once I would schedule one child for Monday, one for Wednesday, and one for Friday. Each girl would get an hour or so alone with me to work on any lessons they needed help with, to vent about problems, or simply read a book together. This alone time with mom or dad is very important so that each child feels special and knows they're being heard and recognized.

Take A Time Out -

There will be times when you're ready to pull your hair out, run out the door, or go into your room and cry. The kids won't listen, one is sick, another is punching her sister, your toddler has a crayon up her nose, and you've just about had it. I used to think there was something wrong with me and my kids when I'd read other books on homeschooling and the mothers seemed like something straight out of *The Stepford Wives* movie. Why couldn't I keep my cool? Why were my kids acting like wild hyenas?

The two biggest changes that helped in these areas was the shorter lessons I mentioned and taking a time out when needed. Kids don't have to have you right by their sides every moment during school lessons. If you're feeling frazzled, give them something fun or creative to do while you take a few minutes to walk around the house, putter in the garden, go to your room and do a few minutes of deep breathing exercises, a brief meditation, call a friend, or something else that will help you calm down and recoup your senses.

True, homeschooling has it's challenging moments, but the rewards are more than worth it. Try to be as prepared as possible each day, keep lessons short, spend some individual time with each child, and take a time out when necessary. Over time you'll discover what works best for you and your family and you'll find that your days are far more productive.

Homeschooling Multiple Ages

When I first started homeschooling my youngest was three and the other two were in third grade. It was a challenge wondering how I would present the lessons when there was such an obvious age gap between the older girls and the youngest.

Being able to homeschool my kids allowed me a lot of freedom though. Kids don't have to be pushed ahead when they aren't ready or held back when they are. There were so many times that my older girls would come home from school saying how bored they were but they couldn't move on with their lessons until most of the class had caught up. Other times, they just couldn't wrap their minds around a certain lesson and, instead of the teacher spending extra time with them, they'd just get left behind and overwhelmed. When we're able to teach our own children we can move as quickly or slowly as they need.

So how did I tackle homeschooling multiple ages? I simply presented the exact same assignment for all of my girls, always at the age level of the older girls. In order for my youngest to keep up, I would have separate math classes at first, and taught her to read while the older girls were reading from their books. This may seem unfair or stressful for younger kids, but in reality they catch on faster than we give them credit for. Sure, my littlest one didn't grasp everything all the time, so if she had questions she asked. Kids are great at asking questions! As parents we should be just as eager to answer.

She was able to understand the art, history, science, and any other lessons we were having at the time. Naturally, I would explain it on her level whenever needed or would have her do the same assignment but within her capabilities. For example, when we did creative writing the older girls would write a story and illustrate it, but my youngest would just draw pictures or narrate the story to me and I would write it for her.

In the beginning she did need a bit more help and guidance, but I truly feel that by having her keep up with her older sisters, it allowed her to excel at a rate that many children—especially those in public school—wouldn't have. By the time she was seven she was reading at a high school level. At the age of sixteen she started college and has a very bright future ahead. She has drive and determination that I admire. In her eyes, if she wants something badly enough she knows if she applies herself she can do it.

It's a fine line to walk when teaching multiple ages, but don't be afraid to lump all of your kids together during the lessons then help out where needed. You just might be surprised at how well the younger ones keep up!

Homeschooling Strategies

Though homeschooling your kids takes time, patience, and a whole lot of responsibility, it *can* be fun and creates memories that last a lifetime. There will also be moments when you feel frustrated, trapped in dull routines, or unsure of how to handle a certain situation or child. These are some strategies I used and have worked for me over the years. Homeschooling is definitely trial and error at times, so don't kick yourself if one thing doesn't work and don't be reluctant to try something else.

1. Even if you shelled out a lot of money or spent a lot of time creating a curriculum and it just isn't working for you and your kids, don't be afraid to change it. You may have to toss the whole thing out and do something totally different, or keep some parts of your current curriculum and round it out with new things. If you aren't sure where to start, check out some homeschooling resources online and read reviews of various curriculums and books so you don't feel like you're walking blindly into this.

I used some workbooks, especially when it came to math, to help fill in the gaps of the curriculum I created myself. However, it took some time before I found out what clicked with all of my kids. You can't stick to something nobody enjoys or is simply too dry or tedious. Homeschooling can and should be enjoyable.

2. Every child is different so try to tailor the lessons to each one accordingly. I mentioned that I taught all of my girls at the same level and the same subjects, with a few tweaks here and there. I also kept the learning styles of my kids in mind as well. For

example, one of my daughters liked writing much better than drawing, another liked being more active, and one enjoyed crafts.

To satisfy the needs of each child, I would do something like this: Say we were learning about Greek mythology, I'd have one daughter write up a report, one draw or paint a detailed picture, and one act out her own one-person play. This way they got to express their individuality yet I knew they all grasped what they were learning. Trying to force our kids into our own learning style just won't work. I love writing, but imagine if I had my "artist" or "actress" sit down and write an essay? They'd quickly get bored and frustrated.

3. Start classes in the morning rather than the afternoon. I would be sure my kids had breakfast and a few minutes to themselves to do whatever they wanted until they were fully awake. We'd then start classes, usually around 9am, but adjust the time to your own family's schedule. Kids are most alert in the morning. There were times when I had doctor's appointments or something else that needed tending to early in the morning and we'd try to tackle school in the afternoon but it seldom worked out well. The kids were already getting antsy, they'd hear the other kids getting home from school and wanted to play outside, and I'd be in a rush as well since my own work, housecleaning and dinner were starting to creep into my mind. Setting aside morning's specifically for school time works the best for most families.

4. Don't feel pressured to teach all subjects each day of the week. My kids enjoyed longer sessions of fewer subjects rather than

trying to squeeze in 5-7 subjects each day. I would often do something like this:

Monday - History, Science (animals)
Tuesday - Geography, Creative Writing, Math
Wednesday - Language Arts, Science (space)
Thursday - Math, Art
Friday - Music, Science

You may choose to cover one subject several times a week or only once a week. We've been programmed during our own schooling that you need to cover all topics multiple times per week. Why? As long as your kids are spending quality time with these subjects and as long as they're truly grasping it, why go over and over and over it?

If you find that covering a topic only once a week doesn't work for your children, try it twice a week. You want to keep things fresh, interesting and relaxed, so try not to squeeze in too many subjects in one day. You could teach one subject for 30 minutes then let the kids work on it for another 30 minutes by themselves before moving on to the next topic. This worked out well for me since they could jump into their homework right after learning the information and I could help whoever needed it. We had school lessons at the dining room table and I'd work in the kitchen while the kids were studying so they knew I was right there if they needed me.

It will be rare when things are smooth sailing with kids, so staying flexible and trying different strategies is important to running a happy, harmonious homeschool.

Socializing Your Homeschooler

This particular subject always puzzled me since people were always so worried that, because my kids weren't in public school, then that surely meant they were being kept in a cave away from all of humanity. In other words, they weren't being socialized and would somehow grow up to be socially inept, awkward, or weird. Just because kids aren't in a traditional classroom doesn't mean they aren't around other kids or adults. Besides their family, which I fully believe counts as socializing, there are usually plenty of kids in the neighborhood. Even if you don't live near many other children, there are a lot of other ways to be sure your kids are socialized.

How Much Socialization?

That's up to each family to decide. My kids would play with the neighborhood children just fine. If there hadn't been so many kids living nearby what would I have done then? Well, I honestly wouldn't have worried about it. It's not like kids will grow up with some fatal flaw if they aren't around other children every single day.

Rather than worrying about socializing your kids enough, why not switch things a bit and ask if you're socializing them right? Even kids in public schools aren't always getting the right kind of interaction with other children. There's bullying, cliques, ostracizing, etc. Who wants that for their child? I know I didn't. Once you've been homeschooling for awhile and have relaxed into it you don't question yourself and your choices as much--

though there are still times when you will!

Why Is It Important To Socialize Our Kids?

The answer is pretty simple; so they can develop their own identity, proper behavior, social skills, and values. Isn't this what we teach our kids on a daily basis though? We show them how to behave, we teach them family values, and want them to learn how to get along with others when we aren't around to guide them every moment.

When I compare my homeschooled children with my public schooled older daughters, I can clearly see the homeschooled kids have grown up to be better communicators, are able to set personal boundaries, and have their own identities. I owe this all to the fact that since they were taught at home they were given a safe place and plenty of time to learn these things rather than being thrown right into it.

Getting Enough Socialization

If you aren't sure your kids are getting enough socialization, a few things you can do is sign your children up for sports, martial arts, music lessons, and youth groups. All of my kids were in martial arts classes and they loved it. They got to get in some physical activity, built self-esteem and confidence, learned to protect themselves, and interacted with other children.

Going against the grain and choosing to homeschool your children will always raise opposing viewpoints in those who choose to send their kids to public school. It doesn't mean they're right and you're wrong, you've simply chosen to school your children in the way that feels right for you. Don't let the thought of your kids not getting enough socialization stop you or worry you. There are many ways for children to interact with others without having to be in a traditional school setting.

Learning Opportunities Are Everywhere

Although I usually worked right through any illness, there was one time when a really awful flu bug knocked me right off my feet. The first day was the worst so I just let my kids have the day off and figured we could make up the work another day. That's just one of the great things about homeschooling; you can do it on your schedule and take days off when you need to or want to.

By the second day I finally felt I would survive, but still didn't have the mental strength to put any lessons or homework plans together. Instead, I told my kids to do some research on the flu virus. They could look information up in the encyclopedias we had. I gave instructions for them to write a report, draw a diagram, and discuss preventive measures so we could avoid the next flu bug that would surely come around. After giving them the instructions I went to lie down and could hear them busily working downstairs in the kitchen/classroom.

What did my kids come up with? Actually, I was pleasantly surprised by how seriously they took the assignments. With Mom dead to the world it would have been so easy for them to spend the day watching TV or playing video games rather than doing any work. However, the fact that I rarely get that sick probably had them worried, and perhaps curious too. What on earth could have attacked Mom so badly that she didn't even have the strength to lift a pencil?

Each of the girls wrote a report on the flu virus. One chose to focus on the Spanish Flu epidemic of 1918 and how it killed an estimated 50 million people worldwide. Another wrote about causes of the flu and preventive measures such as keeping the immune system strong and washing hands—there's a novel idea for kids! The youngest couldn't write an entire report since she was only five, but she wrote a few simple sentences that showed me she absorbed the information her older sisters had shared with her.

They drew carefully labeled diagrams of the flu virus, though my youngest chose to draw a picture of what she thought a flu virus would look like if it were a super-villain. It was very imaginative!

As a homeschooling parent, you can turn almost any situation into a learning opportunity. Instead of stressing over how you'll come up with lessons to keep the kids interested, stand back and take a look at some everyday things that can become homework for the day. You'll be surprised at what you can come up with. Later on in the book I'll share more ideas with you.

Self-Paced Learning

In a moment I'll talk about how I homeschooled my kids using the Charlotte Mason method. I found it to be very thorough yet relaxed at the same time. It also gave me the opportunity to let my kids do a lot of the assignments on their own without me hovering over them every moment or answering a long list of questions that I knew they could answer on their own if they thought about it for awhile.

I would simply make a curriculum schedule for the week, get them started in the morning, then go about and do the things I needed to do around the house. Since I worked from home, this way of teaching was incredibly freeing for me. I was within earshot if someone got stuck, but they learned at their own pace and didn't have many problems.

I did have to be present for other lessons, such as when they needed help with crafts or cooking, though I enjoyed it too so it wasn't much of a sacrifice and I considered it family bonding time. However, the kids could read by themselves and I would hand them a spelling list to memorize, along with other lessons.

Allowing my kids to work in this manner was helpful in a few ways. It gave them a sense of pride being able to work on their own without Mom always looking over their shoulders. It also allowed time for me to get my work done or just relax when I was down to my last nerve or simply exhausted. When you're tired, worried, or stressed, the last thing you need is to answer a thousand questions because your kids have grown so used to you always being right at their elbow.

By giving them some space and teaching them to respect my space, it's allowed them to become self-sufficient young women. They always try to solve a problem on their own first before coming to me for input. Sure, sometimes I miss the days when they were small and needed me for everything, but I can see that my methods have helped us all to become stronger and more independent.

As a homeschooling parent you don't need to be right there on the spot every moment during classes. Give your kids more self-paced learning lessons and you'll see their independence grow while you're able to unwind or get a few things done in the process.

Keep Diligent Records

While homeschooling I had to meet with the school board a few times a year so they could look over my girls' progress. I always dreaded that in the beginning because, I must admit, there was an occasion or two when I wasn't prepared. I didn't bring the right papers, couldn't show enough of certain lessons, and so forth. Don't get caught like a deer in the headlights like I did, be sure you keep diligent records!

There's software you can use to keep track of your homeschooling records. Though I never used software, here are some websites that offer free programs that might be of value to you:

Homeschool Tracker Basic Edition
P.E.R (Plan, Educate, Record)
Homeschool Skedtrack™

During my homeschool journey I found software programs to be unnecessary and just one more thing to think about. Following are a few of the easiest ways I found to keep homeschooling records.

Accordion Folders

Get one accordion folder for each of your children and store their homework assignments, reports, drawings and so forth in them. I like the accordion files since they have several pockets. You can have one pocket for writing and spelling, one for science, one for history, etc. It keeps things organized and easy to find. I bought colored folders and assigned one color per child. This made it easier to pick up the right folder and tuck the pages in it. Keep the folders within easy reach so you're sure to put their work in it rather than sticking the papers on a shelf and forgetting about them. Be sure to date all of the papers as well.

Keep A Notebook

Buy a simple 8x11 spiral bound notebook and write down the day's date and the assignments your kids did. Make notes on any field trips, experiments, projects, books being read, etc. You can also make a note of how many hours the kids had homeschool each day since some states require that you keep track of this as well.

Photo Album

Whenever you go on field trips, are doing interesting experiments, putting on plays, or group activities, be sure to take pictures and keep them in a photo album. Not only will this be fun to look through over the years, but you can use it as proof for the school board as well.

In the beginning I cast all cares to the wind and jumped into homeschooling without doing much record keeping. When the state sent me a list of everything I had to bring in I was stressed to the max trying to scramble and get things organized and make proper notes. Don't let this happen to you! All it takes is a couple of minutes each day to make a few notes and stick some papers into the folders, yet it will save you a lot of time and worry when and if you need to meet with the school board. All you'll need to do is bring the folders, photos, and notebook and show them the work as they ask for it. No sweat!

Dealing With Naysayers

Many times, the moment you even start talking about wanting to homeschool your children, every naysayer within earshot will pipe in with their good-willed advice--usually about how terrible it will be for you and your kids. They warn you that you'll go insane having the kids around the house all the time, that they won't get a proper education, "what do you know about teaching kids?", and, "how will they get enough socializing?"

There are many other bits of advice and warnings you'll hear, but all it boils down to is they're your kids and you're the one who should make the decision to homeschool based on your own values and beliefs. It can be difficult because you may not feel absolutely confident all the time and you might actually start believing them. It can be very demoralizing. So how do you deal with these people--family members, friends, neighbors, strangers--who seem so much against you homeschooling?

Have Confidence In Your Decision

You made the decision to homeschool your children due to your own beliefs, values, morals and reasons. Whether you choose to do so for spiritual reasons, if you feel your kids aren't getting a proper education, if you want to move to a rural area, or are tired of sending your children to overcrowded "kiddy prisons", be confident in the fact that your reasons are valid and you shouldn't have to defend your right to homeschool.

Be A Gentle Listener

Arguing with people about how homeschooling is better than public schooling or becoming defensive will just make things worse. Most people have been led to believe that a parent couldn't possibly be a worthy teacher. After all, shouldn't you have a degree? Of course not! However, the general public is under the false assumption that homeschooled children are lacking in some way. The key here is to gently listen to their opinions and explain your thoughts on the subject then let it go. You aren't trying to convert them and they certainly won't convert you. It will be a no-win situation if you allow their criticism to get you on the defensive. Keep in mind that when someone is insecure with their own beliefs they'll often attack others. Secure people tend to be a lot more understanding, relaxed, and accepting.

Find A Support System

The easiest way to find others who can support you is to locate homeschooling groups in your area. These are families, much like yours, who have decided to teach from home and have probably seen, heard, and been through many of the pitfalls you have and will be. Finding out how they dealt with various issues can be a tremendous comfort in times of stress and confusion. In time you'll be able to offer new homeschooling families moral support as well.

A couple of websites that offer links to homeschooling support groups by state are:

Homeschool World
HSLDA
Secular Homeschool

There will always be people who will want to prove you wrong and tear down every reason why you decided to homeschool. Instead of defending yourself and feeling outnumbered, know in your heart that what you're doing is what you believe is best for your children. What others think and say shouldn't matter.

Year-Round Or Summers Off?

Some parents decide to teach their kids year-round (as I did) and others take the summers off as they do in traditional public schools. The reason I chose to school year-round is because it was a good habit for us to be in and I could make our classes shorter since we did them all year long. For me, this equaled less stress and more stability. I try to live by the no-sweat rule! Also, we could take our vacations during off-season which was a lot cheaper.

Another good homeschooling schedule is to take a month off three times a year. Then again, you may prefer to take summers off. Whatever you decide is up to you, but try various schedules to see what works best for you and your family.

Even if you do take long stretches of time off, a month or longer, you can still give your kids learning opportunities. One really good strategy is to have them do some unschooling and choose a subject they'd like to learn more about and immerse themselves in it. One of my daughters became fascinated with koalas so I had her read up on them and we visited the zoo so she could observe them in real life. She wrote a story about a koala and watched many videos online. She became a virtual koala expert! Another one of my daughters got into skateboarding and did pretty well. You could even find educational computer games they can play during your off-time, such as learning some basic words or greetings in a foreign language, or watching kids movies in a foreign language.

Everyone needs a break, even if you do decide to homeschool year-round, but that doesn't mean your children have to become lazy or bored. There are plenty of fun ways for them to learn without making it feel like a chore or "real school."

The Charlotte Mason Method

As I've mentioned, after watching my two oldest girls struggle with public school due to boredom and friction with "the cool kids", I decided to homeschool my three youngest. It was an easy decision, but creating my own curriculum was often confusing. I didn't want to use the traditional Christian homeschool programs such as Alpha Omega and Abeka. Aside from the fact that they're quite costly, I found them to be more stringent than what I was looking for.

While doing some research on homeschooling methods I came upon the Charlotte Mason Method. It seemed very free-spirited, at least to me, yet at the same time the kids would be getting a solid education. Far more than what they were receiving in the public school system.

Charlotte Mason

Charlotte Mason was an educator in the 1800's who believed that children learned best through the use of living books, art, and nature. She has inspired many parents to homeschool their children, myself included. If it hadn't been for her books and their guidance, I probably would have thrown in the towel and bought a costly prepackaged curriculum for my girls.

Living Books

"Living books" aren't like dull textbooks. Instead, a living book is one where the reader feels she's immersed in the story, living out the scenes the author has written about. These books spark creativity and keep children so interested they aren't even aware they're learning. There are website devoted to the Charlotte Mason way of teaching and they offer hundreds of these types of living books for sale. They can even be checked out through your local library. There are many subjects to choose from, so no matter how many children you're homeschooling or how different their interests, you're sure to find something they enjoy. These books cover everything from fine arts and science, to spelling.

Interesting For Everyone

As parents, we should have the right to homeschool our children in the way see fit, as long as they're actually getting an education. With the Charlotte Mason Method I had fun right alongside my girls. Best of all, it works for all ages. I used her approach from preschool and all through their teens, and let me tell you, it doesn't get boring!

Think back to when you were in school, especially high school. Those long, boring lectures with the teacher droning on and dry textbooks. You won't find that with Ms. Mason's program. She believed that children needed a well-rounded education with an emphasis on music, art and literature.

In this day and age though the public sees little use for these fine arts and old classics. Our kids are forced to start taking algebra before they're ready and high-tech fields are stuffed down their throats. Yes, these subjects have their place, but there's a lot to be said for gentle learning. My girls have become passionate learners, hard workers, and responsible young ladies. Contrary to what most people think about homeschooled kids, my daughters are outgoing and quite social. Their friends are always amazed at their level of intelligence. I owe it all to them being homeschooled.

If you'd like to find out more about the Charlotte Mason Method there are many great websites online that have information about her methods, living books, curriculum, lessons and more. I've included some of my favorite websites below. I urge you to give it a try, it will make homeschooling fun, memorable and very low stress.

Simply Charlotte Mason
Living Books Curriculum
The Homeschool Mom - Charlotte Mason Method
Ambleside Online- "A free homeschool curriculum designed to be as close as possible to the curriculum that Charlotte Mason used in her own private and correspondence schools."
Design Your homeschool

Using Art Journals

Notebooks are a wonderful way to keep track of science, language arts, history, creative writing, and other assignments. It keeps things neat and tidy, and there aren't loose papers all over the place. I quickly discovered that having one big three-ring binder filled with notebook paper and dividers just didn't work out well. The papers often tore out and the binders were heavy and clumsy for my kids to use.

Instead, by purchasing color-coded notebooks and writing each child's name on the front with a big permanent ink marker, it kept things more organized. My kids didn't feel as overwhelmed as they did before when having to drag out that five-pound binder. We used one color for each subject: Red for history, purple for language arts, yellow for creative writing, green for science, etc.

I also bought each one of my girls a notebook to use as an art journal. You can get these spiral bound notebooks at any craft or art supply store such as Michael's. The pages are thick and unlined. Each week we would focus on one artist and his or her life and works. Three of our favorite books to use were:

Discovering Great Artists: Hands On Art For Children In The Styles Of The Great Masters
DK's Art: A World History
Great Artists: The Lives of 50 Great Painters Explored Through Their Work

What I would do is have the kids read about a great artist on Monday and we would go through our art books and look at some of their masterpieces. Tuesday they would write a report of the artist in their Art Journal. They didn't have to write anything word-for-word or something dull or dry, they could write about interesting things they learned about the artist, funny happenings in their lives, tragedies, their pets, or whatever each one of my children remembered most.

On Wednesday we would choose a project then go out and buy any materials necessary. Usually we had everything we needed at home and we did try to stick with sketching, pastels, watercolors, and acrylics. We quickly found out that oil painting wasn't a good project to tackle until the kids were older. I talk about that lesson next.

Thursday and Friday would be the days my children would work on their art project. They could either copy something one of these great masters created, or pursue their own project using the artist's style such as impressionism or cubism.

By keeping this art journal, at the end of the school year each child ended up with a very thick notebook filled with information on some of the world's greatest artists in history, along with their own renditions of famous masterpieces.

Lesson Learned - Avoid Oil Paints

I'm a pretty laid back person and encourage my children to always try new things. Not much irritates me or has me worrying over how white my carpets look or how clean the floors are. However, several years ago we tried an art project that made me wish I had a time machine that would transport us back to the day before I came up with this bright idea.

Since I'm a big fan of the Charlotte Mason method, I loved teaching my children about classical music, books, and artists. A moment ago I briefly talked about one of our favorite books; *DK Art: A World History*. This monster packs 712 pages and weighs a hefty 6.1 pounds. Each week we would choose a famous painter or sculptor, I would read about his or her life then we'd set out to make our own works of art.

One week I decided to focus on Renoir. I went to our local Michael's to purchase canvas boards, oil paints, thinner, and linseed oil. Right away I noticed that these supplies were much more expensive than pastels, watercolors, or acrylics. I wanted my kids to have experiences with as many art mediums as possible so I went ahead and made the purchase.

Knowing that oil paints were messy, before we started the project I laid down newspapers and had the kids put on their most ragged T-shirts. As my girls each picked which painting they wanted to duplicate, I prepared their paints and tended to my own project as well.

To say that oil paints are messy is an understatement. Try as we might, we still got the paint everywhere. My youngest dropped her canvas and it landed, paint-side down, right on the dog. It took several days for the paintings to dry, and the colors looked very muddy. Nobody was satisfied with their work and our kitchen table still bears the marks of our failed attempt at oil painting. Although I thought we were thorough in cleaning the brushes, by the time we went to try a new project the bristles were dry and stuck together.

Over the years I've collected a nice collection of wannabe Picasso's, Van Gogh's, Warhol's, and Cassatt's, just to name a few. But after our experience with oil paints, we stuck to acrylics and water colors.

Creative Writing Prompts

My kids always enjoyed creative writing. They come by it naturally since I've loved writing ever since I could hold a crayon, though I soon learned that walls weren't to be used as giant pieces of paper. Thankfully, my kids never had the urge to apply colored scribbling to our bare white walls. Even with my youngest, all I had to do is hand her a tablet and a pack of crayons then offer her a creative writing prompt. Back then she could only draw stick figures and gibberish, but it was still good practice for when she got older.

Coming up with prompts got to be tricky if I tried to do it on the spot, so during a creative moment when my kids were outside playing I took a pack of note cards, a black marker, and a recipe file box then set out to create 100 creative writing prompts. I figured I could choose one each day and all three girls could write about the same subject, or they could sift through the box and find something that sparked their imagination.

The easiest way to come up with a variety of writing prompts was to think of them in categories. For instance, I thought about fairytales and came up with suggestions like:

*As a princess, this is what my average day is like.
*I found a magic lamp...
*A big dragon walked up to my castle today...
*I have a rainbow colored horse that flies.
*If I were a fairy...

While fantasy writing suggestions were some of my girls' favorites, I didn't want them to only focus on magical lives. There were also seasonal prompts to help them think in the near future or recall some of their favorite memories.

*The funniest thing that happened last summer was...
*This winter I'd really like to...
*The greatest garden in the world would be...
*During the fall, the most fun I have is when...

I also wanted to get my kids to think deeply about the world in general and focus on others beside themselves. Children don't often think about the fact that there are plenty of negative things happening in the world. Although I didn't want to depress my kids or cause them stress, I offered some prompts that would get them to at least think about being proactive when it comes to some of the world's issues.

*This is how I would end world hunger...
*If people keep cutting down trees, our world will...
*The day in the life of a homeless person...
*If I were president, the first thing I would do...

It's good to have a wide variety of writing suggestions for your kids to choose from. Creating many topics that will jumpstart their imaginations, come up with solutions, or simply ponder over will offer them the chance to explore their thoughts, feelings, opinions, and dreams.

Other Countries - A Whole Curriculum

When first homeschooling my girls we lived in Baltimore and the school board is pretty relaxed on the curriculum. You can use traditional curriculums and workbooks or create your own, as long as the children are given a thorough education. Truthfully, my kids were bored to death with workbooks and textbooks so I decided to create a curriculum that would really stimulate their senses.

I bought a world map and taped it to the dining room wall—our makeshift classroom for many years. Each week I would choose one of the girls, have her close her eyes, spin her around a few times, then told her to put her finger on the map anywhere. Wherever she pointed, that would be our subject for the coming week.

One time my youngest pointed to Alaska. We took a trip to the library—an important resource for homeschooling parents—and chose several books on Alaska, its history, the people, the language, foods, crafts, and we even found a CD with Inuit music. Over the weekend I put this into lessons for the week which focused on Geography, Geology, Anthropology, Art, Language, History, Music, and so on. We would learn some of their phrases, cook up some food, and in the background I would play the CD during lessons.

This was incredibly fun, even for me, and the girls stayed interested all through elementary and middle school. Now that they're grown I can see how our other countries whole-curriculum lessons have broadened their horizons. My youngest wants to become a photojournalist and travel, one of my other daughters is taking multiple language courses, and another is taking classes in foreign management.

Teaching your kids doesn't have to be boring, nor do you have to jump around from lesson to lesson. By offering them a curriculum that embraces one country or topic at a time you can actually tackle many subjects at once that blend seamlessly into one another. They'll learn about other countries and cultures in great detail and have fun doing it. Most people don't have money to travel the globe, but this is truly the next best thing.

Whole Curriculum Gardening

Once spring arrives most states start to thaw out and warm up. This is an excellent time to start a garden, no matter how small, and teach your kids about botany, art, vocabulary, water conservation, nutrition, and so much more.

I'm a firm believer in getting the most bang for my buck and the most use out of every moment. Each lesson you teach your children can incorporate many subjects, not just the most obvious one at hand. Gardening is no different.

The house we lived in at the time had a nice back and front yard, but even when we lived in an apartment we still did container gardening. No matter how little space you have you can enjoy beautiful flowers, fresh herbs, and juicy tomatoes.

A Whole Curriculum

There are very few homeschool activities that are as fun or rewarding as home gardening. Even on a tight budget it doesn't take much money to buy a few packets of seeds and potting soil. As the plants grow, kids can keep a journal of their progress, drawing pictures of the developing plants, labeling them, coloring or painting their drawings, and writing about the various elements present. What's the weather like each day? Are you growing the plants indoors or outdoors? How much watering do they need?

A spelling list can be created out of plant names—both common and Latin—plant parts, and everything that goes along with gardening. I usually came up with a master list of at least 50 words at the beginning of the week and gave my kids 10 words from the list each day. You can recycle the list for an entire month, or come up with new words.

Depending on what you're growing, you can look up the history, nutritional values, recipes, art projects and so much more. Instead of trying to put together many separate lessons, incorporate your main project into every school subject you can, this way your kids are getting a thorough education in the subject at hand and you don't have to stress yourself trying to come up with many varied lessons.

Getting Started

The first time you try out home gardening things may not go as well as next year and the year after, which is why keeping a journal will help. Some plants will thrive in your area, while others may wilt and die within weeks. Other plants will need more shade or more sun. Following guidance in a gardening book or online site is helpful, but it could never take the place of personal experience.

For starting seeds, one of the best things we've found is cardboard egg cartons. This is a great way to reuse something instead of throwing it away and adding to our overly packed landfills.

Simply fill each section of the carton with soil, poke a shallow hole in each area with your finger, add two or three seeds, then cover them up with soil. Add just a bit of water to moisten the dirt but not drown the seeds.

Check each day to see if the seeds need more water and be sure to place them in a sunny location, such as a table near a window. You can put the cardboard egg cartons on a baking sheet or something else to protect the table or counter from any water damage.

Transplanting

When the seeds have sprouted and are about three inches high you can then transplant them outdoors in your garden or in bigger pots. As time goes by your children will be able to pick flowers or vegetables and use herbs in cooking that they grew themselves. Ever since we started growing our own tomatoes my kids are amazed at how terrible the ones from the store taste.

You can make your garden as simple or intensive as you'd like, though starting out with something easy and hearty is best in the beginning. If you find that your kids like gardening, you can increase the size of your garden next year. We got so much into gardening that we had a dozen different vegetables and herbs growing at once. Children feel proud when they know they're contributing to the household, and growing veggies is a fun and easy way for them to do so.

Our favorite book to use was:

Postage Stamp Gardening: Grow Tons Of Vegetables In Small Spaces

What I enjoyed about this book is the authors, Duane and Karen Newcomb, make it look so easy. And it is! No matter if you've got a few pots, a 4-foot square area in your yard, or something a bit bigger, you can easily grow lots of vegetables and you don't have to be a rocket scientist to do it. That's what made it so much fun. Kids learn best when they're enjoying themselves, and we parents teach best when we're enjoying ourselves.

A few great websites for knowing when to plant outdoors in your area is:
Garden.org - USDA Hardiness Zone Finder
Almanac.com - Planting A Garden (Lots of great information on this site!)

Whole Curriculum History

As you've read over the past few pages, I like to get as much "across the curriculum" learning out of a subject as I can. Why have separate reading, history, art, writing, and science projects when you can take one subject you're currently studying and make it work for all areas? This is being frugal with your time, and kids can really immerse themselves in the topic at hand rather than having their minds jump from one completely different subject to another.

Another positive aspect of taking one topic and applying as many assignments to it as possible is you can often let children work on their own. Whether you choose a certain country, a classic novel, or a time period in history as a whole curriculum, you can be certain your homeschooled children are getting a solid education.

For example, one time I chose Ancient Egypt to use for a weeklong subject. I set aside a few hours on the weekend developing the assignments and gathering any books and supplies we needed, and I made certain that I fit the subject of Ancient Egypt into as many school subjects as possible. This is a rough outline of how I did this and titles of the books I used:

*History – Spend A Day In Ancient Egypt
*Science – Secrets Of The Mummies
*Anthropology – Discuss ancient burial routines compared with present day burials.
*Art – Hieroglyphics: Use plaster of Paris to make a rough slab

then have kids "paint" the slab with cold coffee to make the plaster look aged. Have children use black paint to write hieroglyphs that spell out their name—or close to it.

*Reading – <u>Gods and Pharaohs from Egyptian Mythology</u>

*Writing – Have children write about what they've learned. They can either write their own creative writing story of what it would be like to live in Ancient Egypt, or have children copy passages from their reading book. This last method is often used with the Charlotte Mason program.

For math you could either show the children the Ancient Egyptians' counting method or simply use a math workbook. I'll admit, I used math workbooks for the most part since it's a subject that just about gives me hives.

As you can see, by taking one interesting subject you can offer your children an education that goes beyond just a simple history lesson.

Teaching Science

Though you can easily incorporate science into your whole curriculum strategy, there may be times when you want to solely focus on this subject. The problem with teaching science to homeschoolers is that we don't have access to the same equipment and supplies that public and private schools do. As a homeschooling parent it's necessary to think outside the box and not corner yourself into believing you need to dissect frogs and have a chemistry set to properly study science. In fact, science is such a broad subject that it includes far more than lab lessons. We also want to make learning fun. After all, if our kids are enjoying themselves they'll learn faster and retain the information and we'll feel a lot less stressed in the process.

What are some things you can do to easily teach your children science while trying to incorporate fun at the same time?

Trash The Textbooks

Better yet, don't waste your money on them in the first place. Do you remember being in school and reading those long, boring, dull books? It felt like your brain would explode or slowly slip into a coma. Text books are very expensive, and most adults hate reading them, yet alone getting kids to immerse themselves in those dry passages. Instead, find books on subjects you and your kids are interested in and make short notes on some interesting facts and information. No matter how old your children are, they'll learn better if they can use as many of their senses as possible, so keep this in mind. Find books with a lot of interesting pictures and condensed bits of information. (DK books are fabulous for this.)

Think about it, what will kids remember longer and get more excited about, a book that's just one long paragraph after another, or a book with real pictures and short paragraphs with pertinent information?

Activities

Science is an area where there are loads of books that offer fun and easy activities. Whether you make homemade *Silly Putty*, raise fish, grow plants, dissect a squid you bought at the market, test your tap water, go stargazing, or keep track of the weather, the list is nearly endless.

Some of the best books we used were:

Hands On Grossology: The Science Of Really Gross Experiments
Silly Science: Strange And Startling Projects To Amaze Your Family And Friends
Quick Science: Experiments You Can Do In A Minute

As you can see, we enjoyed a lot of hands-on activities. We covered a lot of other science subjects when we did our whole curriculum studies. I already talked about gardening, Ancient Egypt, and other countries.

It doesn't matter if your kids are 5 or 15, we all learn when our senses are stimulated rather than being bored.

Field Trips

One of the best, and usually free, field trips you can go on when exploring sciences topics is to museums. Many cities have hands-on science museums for kids where they can interact with various displays that range from earthquakes and ant farms to how electricity works and sound waves. Even museums that aren't hands-on can be interesting for kids to explore. When we lived in California we would go to the Natural History Museum and my kids loved it. When we moved to Baltimore we would visit Washington DC and the Smithsonian museums there.

To find museums in your area, you can check out these websites:

American Association Of Museums
Wikipedia: List Of Museums In The United States
Exploring Abroad (this site lists museums worldwide)

Go Online

Even if you can't get to a museum or even the library to check out some science books, there are plenty of great websites that can supplement your science lessons. Many of these websites have videos, games, quizzes, ideas for easy experiments, and downloadable content. Some of the best websites are:

Discovery Kids which features games, quizzes, activities, and a "Tell Me" section that covers ten different subjects such as Earth, Health, Science, Space and Machines.

Kids.gov offers information on how to become president, American history, games and activities, branches of the government, art, money, science, and so much more. Best of all, it covers grades K-8 so there's something for everyone.

Try Science has many fun experiments you can do from home like making your own cheese with only milk, vinegar and a coffee filter! Or, make musical coat hangers or find out what your lung capacity it. There are also great ideas for field trips.

Chemistry Activities For Kids at About.com Here you'll find everything from making bubbles and growing crystals to putting together a chemistry kit for home and throwing science parties. A wealth of information for all ages, straight through high school.

Learning science doesn't have to boring or expensive if you keep these tips in mind. All it takes is a few interesting books, websites, and visits to your local museums. I always felt that if I didn't enjoy teaching (and learning!) along with my kids then what was the point in homeschooling? When you're not having a good time then it's time to go over your curriculum and find ways to inject a healthy dose of fun.

Making Math Fun

This was always a tough subject for me. I'm not a numbers person by any means. My talents tend to run toward the creative side rather than mathematical. For the most part I used math workbooks and it carried us far in our homeschooling journey, but I also used a few elementary math games to add more enjoyment. The following games and strategies are simple and will actually help children grasp things like addition, subtraction, multiplying, dividing, decimals and fractions much easier than if they solely work from a book. Remember, most everyone learns faster and retains the information longer if they're *doing* something rather than simply reading about it.

Real Life Math

One of the easiest and best things to do is to make math part of everyday life, this way kids don't feel like they're being taught. Instead, you simply take advantage of situations where you can sneak in a math lesson without kids knowing it.

At the store - I would usually take my kids to the grocery store with me and point out various things such as: "Look girls, the cereal you like is on sale this week. Last week it was $2.99 a box and now it's $1.99. How much money are we saving per box?" Or I would point out two identical types of cereal that were about the same price but one weighed more than the other and I'd ask them to tell me which is the better deal. Also, I would show them two smaller boxes of cereal that were on sale and a much bigger box that wasn't and ask them if getting two small boxes on sale was cheaper than the bigger box not being on sale.

With smaller purchases I would have one of my children count out the money and hand it to the cashier so they got comfortable with handling money as well.

In the kitchen - When following a recipe I would typically double it since there were seven of us in the family. I'd make sure that I'd have one child each day help me cook and ask them to read the recipe if they were old enough to do so or I'd read it out loud if they were still too young. I would then say, "Since we're doubling it, how many eggs will we need? How many cups of milk?" and so on. This is great for teaching fractions as well. Sometimes I would hide one of the measuring cups and we'd have to use another size. I might tuck away the one-cup measurer and we'd have to use the half-cup and they'd really have to think about how much flour, milk, or whatnot to use. I did the same with the measuring spoons at times. Sneaky? Yes, but they learned quickly and found solving these puzzles to be fun.

These were just a couple of examples in using math in everyday instances.

Counting Numbers

I never bought a book, flashcards, or kits that helped my kids to learn how to count. Why do that when there are so many opportunities for kids to learn this while doing chores, helping out with dinner, or putting things in the shopping cart? If there's one or more of anything, kids can count it.

I remember one time after doing laundry one of my daughters was helping me to fold socks. As we tossed the folded socks into a basket, ready to make the rounds to everyone's dresser, she counted them. It was also fun for her to toss them into the basket, so it was more of a game than any math lesson!

Recognizing and Writing Numbers

Teaching younger children to recognize and write numbers can also be turned into a game. I lost count of how many times we watched <u>Sesame Street: 123 Count With Me</u>. All of my kids loved it, even when they were a bit older. A few other things we did to help them learn to recognize and write numbers was to give them a paper where I wrote the numbers 0 - 9. I would then tell them to copy the numbers on their own paper while saying them out loud then turn the numbers into funny characters. They drew top hats, googly eyes, polka dots, monster fangs, fancy shoes, and more on the numbers. I also did this when they were learning the alphabet. My youngest loved this project and never tired of it. In fact, even on non-school days she'd work on these number or letter doodles. Kids can also make numbers out of clay, write them on the sidewalk with chalk, even draw them with their finger on the peanut butter in their sandwiches--messy, but fun.

Higher/Lower

The game of War is another fun and easy game that uses nothing more than a deck of cards. Shuffle the deck and deal the cards out face down, one at a time, to each player. When all of the cards have been dealt, each person turns over the top card of their own deck. The person with the highest card gets all the cards that have been turned over. In the end, the one with the most cards wins.

Simple game, right? And it's a great way for younger kids to learn which numbers are higher and which are lower. Often I'd take out the jokers and face cards, and just use aces through 10s. The game can get rather fast, so in the beginning take your youngest aside and play together just the two of you. Or, have one of your oldest teach the youngest.

Addition/Subtraction/Multiplication

Using one or two sets of dice, decide on what you want your kids to work on. Let's say that today you want them to practice addition and you're working with younger kids. In this instance you might want to use only two dice. The youngest gets to roll first and adds up the sum of both dice. If he gets it correct you can offer a small prize like stickers, pennies, nuts, a gummy candy, or whatever you choose. (Note: Carrot sticks don't work and even grapes only got a lukewarm response. Kids need more of an incentive than healthy veggies or fruits. I learned that lesson fast!)

As your kids get older and better at math you can have them roll four dice and add them up, or add up two of the dice and the other two then subtract those sums from each other. You can also get into multiplication as well. If your kids want to be a bit more competitive and they're around the same age and math level, they can blurt out the answer no matter who rolls. The winner gets a point and the one with the most points wins.

This also works with cards. You can take out jokers and face cards or label the face cards as: Jacks = 11, Queens = 12, Kings = 13. Place the shuffled deck between the kids and have the first one--usually the youngest--take two cards and lay them face up. They can add, subtract, multiply or divide, depending on what you chose for them to practice before the game started. Each child can take their own turn or they can compete.

Odd/Even

Here's where that deck of cards comes in handy once again. Have your child put all the even cards in one pile and all the odd cards in another. This is a very fast and simple idea and works really well if you get a deck of kid-friendly cards that has cute pictures on them.

Counting Higher Numbers

When teaching younger kids to count to higher numbers, even one-hundred and beyond, something that worked with my children was smaller items like jellybeans and macaroni. One year we put small jellybeans in bigger plastic eggs to hand out to their friends in the neighborhood. I had my daughter count out fifty small jellybeans and put them into each egg. She did get bored after the first several eggs, but it was good practice and it didn't feel like homework. Another thing I did was to buy a one pound bag of rigatoni and have her count how many were in the bag as she put each one into a bowl. We'd then cook the pasta and serve it for dinner, so she felt she was helping with the meal and not actually doing a math lesson.

These are just some of the things I used with my kids. Hopefully this has given you some ideas you can try with your own children. There are plenty of good math websites on the internet. The site my kids enjoyed the most is Cool Math 4 Kids. The website has bright neon colors and offers many activities and games. Believe it or not, I sometimes go onto the site just to practice math once in awhile. If you don't use it you'll lose it! Cool Math 4 Kids covers everything from addition and subtraction to pre-algebra and geometry. The Number Monster game is a lot of fun, as is Brain Benders.

If your kids are older they can head on over to the site Cool Math where they cover pre-algebra and even calculus. Just because it's for older kids doesn't mean it's not as much fun as their other website. This one is just as colorful and kids can practice finances, geometry, trig, and even learn how to lower their stress levels. This is one of the best math websites I've ever seen and used.

Now you see that math doesn't have to be focused solely on textbooks and workbooks. If you're children are playing games and helping with family chores, you can sneak in some math lessons without them knowing.

Field Trips

This was something we really enjoyed about homeschooling; going on field trips. When my two older daughters were in public school I noticed that over the years the number of field trips the schools offered went down from three trips per year to one to zero. When you homeschool your kids you can go on as many field trips as you'd like!

Besides getting out of the house for awhile, kids can socialize and learn about art, science, history, nature and more. Don't think you need a lot of money to go on field trips either since many cities have museums that are free on specific days and parks are always free. Even a walk around the block can become a mini-field trip. I've taken my kids to the florist, home repair stores, pharmacies, pet shelters, vacant lots, fabric stores, and other places that don't seem like traditional field trip destinations. The lessons you provide your children are endless and you can come up with some really creative opportunities to teach when and where you least expect it.

When you get back home after a field trip, the lessons don't have to stop. You can discuss the trip, have your kids write stories or reports, draw pictures, do a craft, or ask them to make an entry in their journals. You can start them off with something like, "The best thing about this field trip was...." Or, "Something interesting I learned on this field trip...."

Sometimes, a field trip may spur your kids to study something more in-depth. One time I took my kids to the arboretum to see the various plants, trees, and flowers there. While we were walking around one of my daughter's spotted a robin redbreast on one of the bushes. I'm sure she had seen them before, but for some reason it really piqued her attention and curiosity that day. After the field trip she read all she could about the bird, wrote a poem about it, did a watercolor painting and photographed some in the wild (in our backyard.) I've found that homeschooling my kids kept them wide open to new learning possibilities, many of which they pursued themselves. Rather than fitting them into the tight structure of public school, they were allowed the freedom to think and explore any time they wanted to without being stifled.

Field Trip Ideas

Factories - Many factories offer free tours to families and some give out free samples and souvenirs to take home.

Zoo - Your local zoo or aquarium may be expensive, but they often have family days where they give a deep discount or have free admission. If it's a place your family loves going, you might consider an annual pass. Many times the annual pass pays for itself just after a couple of visits. Keep your eyes open for discounts too. When I lived in Baltimore the aquarium was expensive during the summer months, but around November through February they would have $5 admission on Friday's after 5pm. The attractions in your area may have similar discounts during off-season.

Live Shows - During summer months many parks have free

concerts, plays and cultural events that are absolutely free. We've seen belly dancing, jazz bands, Irish clog dancing, comedians, magicians, and much more at our local parks.

Field trips are an important part of homeschooling though it doesn't have to cost you an arm and a leg. Also, be on the lookout for shorter outings that you can turn into mini-field trips or atypical places like animal shelters, aquarium shops or other stores or shops that can stand in for more traditional field trips.

One Song Cleanup

Homeschooling our kids is rewarding, but it can also be messy. Having children around the house all day long rather than away at school for six or more hours meant that we needed to clean up several times a day rather than just once as I used to when my older girls were in public school.

Parents are notorious for trying to be superheroes and tend to do everything themselves. Whether it's something like vacuuming, doing dishes, a load of wash, or cleaning the cat box, it's often easier to just do it ourselves rather than listening to the kids moan and groan. Not to mention, we often have to prod them a thousand times before they'll get the least little thing done at times.

A good way to handle the messes and stresses of housecleaning is to get the kids involved with it, but in such a way that they actually have fun or at least don't mind helping out. This is where the "One Song Cleanup" comes in.

This small tactic was like a mini-miracle in my life. At the end of the school day there were usually papers, art supplies, and lunch leftovers from the living room to the kitchen, and everyplace in between. It needed to be cleaned up and there sure weren't any volunteers.

What I did was to make a mix CD with fast-paced fun songs my kids liked. When it came time for the One Song Cleanup I'd announce it to the kids, put a song on at random and everyone would work their fastest to get the house in order again. It's amazing at how much work kids can get done within such a short period of time with high-energy music in the background.

This tactic works well for any type of cleaning, not just end of the school day messes. I'd assign each child a room to work on, let the music play, and we were off! Within a few minutes everyone was laughing, breathless, and the house looked pretty good. Of course, it wasn't as pristine as when I did the work myself, but it was passable. Plus, it allowed time for everyone to work toward a common goal and taught my kids responsibility.

Give the One Song Cleanup routine a try and you may find that your kids don't grumble as much when it comes to cleaning. You'll probably find that you're also far less stressed since you won't have to nag them or simply do it all yourself.

Thank You!

I hope you've enjoyed this short book on No Sweat Homeschooling. This path you've taken with your children is one of the most wondrous and memorable you'll ever walk with them. You, as their teacher, are opening new worlds to them and leading them into the future with skills and an education that you and you alone feel will benefit them most. What could be better? Having so much together time with them is fulfilling as well. You'll be able to share in the big and small victories your children go through since you're with them each day rather than sending them off into the arms of strangers.

Yes, homeschooling has its ups and downs. There are days when you'll want to call it off and ship them right back to public classes. If you relax into your role as a homeschooling parent though and keep in mind that nearly every moment of every day offers opportunities for learning, you won't feel nearly as stressed out or lacking.

Thank you for joining me while I shared some of my tips, triumphs and pitfalls. I look forward to sharing future books with you!

If you'd like to share your thoughts and comments about this book, your own homeschooling tips or stories, or have ideas for future books please feel free to contact me at:

AuthorKellyWallace@gmail.com

Other Nonfiction Books By Kelly Wallace

Reprogram Your Subconscious - Get Everything You Want
10 Minutes A Day To A Powerful New Life
True Wealth - Reprogram Your Mind For Financial Success
Unlimited Success
Happiness: Live It Every Day
Soul Mates - Finding And Keeping Mr. Right
Contacting And Working With Your Spirit Guides
Energy Work – Aura Clearing and Healing
Intuitive Tarot
Psychic Living – Developing Your Intuition
Spirit Guides and Healing Energy
Contacting and Working with your Angels
Learn Spell Casting Right Now
How to Cure Candida

About The Author

Kelly Wallace is a typical workaholic—and loves every busy minute of it. Not only is she a single mother and best-selling romance author, but she's also a highly respected self-help author. She travels regularly between Arizona, Texas and Maryland to spend time with loved ones.

Kelly has used the methods she teaches in her nonfiction books to go from two dysfunctional marriages, living in a dilapidated one-bedroom house, and bringing in only $900 a month while supporting and homeschooling five children on her own, to being in a passionate relationship with her soulmate, living in a beautiful home, traveling and making a six-figure income as an author.

Her background consists of more than 20 years experience in:

~ Brief Solution-Based Therapy, Hypnotherapy, Dream Analysis, NLP, Herbology, Aromatherapy, Vitamin and Mineral Therapy, Chakra Therapy, Hand Reflexology, Meditation, Visualization, Assertiveness and Confidence Building.
~ Pastoral Counseling, Relationship Counseling, Psychic

Counseling, Life Coach, Doctor of Divinity.

~ Multi-published author, radio show host, freelance writer, ghostwriter.

~ Previous marketing director and radio show manager for a publishing company.

~ Freelance writer for many blogs, top media content sites and magazines both digital and in print.

You can contact her at:

AuthorKellyWallace@gmail.com

Printed in Great Britain
by Amazon.co.uk, Ltd.,
Marston Gate.